Iphigenia

Euripides was born near Athens between 485 and 480 BC and grew up during the years of Athenian recovery after the Persian Wars. His first play was presented in 455 BC and he wrote some hundred altogether. Nineteen survive – a greater number than those of Aeschylus and Sophocles combined – including *Electra, Hippolytos, Andromache, Ion, Alkestis* and *The Women of Troy*. A year or two before his death he left Athens to lie at the court of the King of Macedon, dying there in 406 BC. Methuen publish all nineteen of his plays in six volumes in their Classical Greek Dramatists series.

Edna O'Brien's novels include *The Country Girls Trilogy, Night, Down by the River* and *In the Forest*. Her plays include *A Pagan Place* (Royal Court Theatre, London); *Virginia* (Haymarket Theatre, Leicester) and *Our Father* (Almeida Theatre, London).

Iphigenia

by

Euripides

Adapted by

Edna O'Brien

Methuen Drama

Published by Methuen 2003

1 3 5 7 9 10 8 6 4 2

First published in 2003 by
Methuen Publishing Limited
215 Vauxhall Bridge Road
London SW1V 1EJ

Methuen Publishing Limited Reg. No. 3543167

A CIP catalogue record for this book is available from the British Library

ISBN 0 413 77381 7

Typeset by SX Composing DTP, Rayleigh, Essex
Printed and bound in Great Britain by
Cox & Wyman Ltd, Reading, Berkshire

Introduction

Euripides was the scourge of his native Athens, his plays
regarded as seditious and corrupting. Born in exile, on the
island of Salamis, in 480 BC, he died in exile in Macedonia
in his mid-seventies. Accounts differ as to the nature of his
death, but chief among them is the hearsay that he was set
upon and torn to death by mad dogs or mad women who
could not tolerate his depiction of them as passionate,
avenging and murderous. His plays shocked public opinion,
offended the critics and ensured that he was overlooked year
after year in the state competitions, with Sophocles and
Aeschylus sharing the laurels. Sophocles was a distinguished
figure who enjoyed public prestige, and Aeschylus could
boast of his prowess in the war against the invading
Persians. Euripides, however, was marginalised even
though, as an able-bodied young man, he would have had
to serve in army and fleet since Athens was vulnerable to
marauders from east and west.

His crimes were legion. He had questioned the prestige of
the state, of pious honour and ancient injunctions, had
portrayed the gods as vicious, merciless, sparring creatures
who gave rein to violent, even insane passions. Medea, who
sent a robe of burning poison to her rival and subsequently
butchered her children, was a heroine whose deeds were a
blight on enlightened Athens, and the official judges of the
annual prize put it at the bottom of the list. Three and a half
centuries later, the historian Aelian said the judges 'were
either ignorant, imbecilic philistines or else bribed.'
Euripides' depiction of women led to scatological rumours
such as that he had learned their abnormal tendencies and
sexual misconduct from everyday experience, that his
mother Clito was an illiterate quack dabbling in herbs,
potions and fortune-telling, moreover he was a cuckold, a
bigamist and a misogynist who lived in rancorous isolation
in a cave. It says much for his inward spirit and dedication
to his calling that he wrote over a hundred plays – nineteen
of which are in existence – and that when he died in
Macedonia, Sophocles, out of a mark of delayed homage for

his great rival, made his chorus wear mourning for the evening performance.

Euripides is the dramatist, along with Shakespeare, who delved most deeply into the doings and passions of men and women. His dramas, while being political, religious and philosophic, are also lasting myths in which the beauty and lamentation of his choruses are in direct contrast with the barbarity of his subjects. As with Shakespeare he found the existing stories and legends too good, too primal, to be abandoned and so he appropriated tales from Homeric times, rewrote them, transformed them and made them a foil for his prodigious imagination so that they serve as staple and forerunner for all drama that came after him. Sophocles' characters can seem stiff, their language elaborate, but Euripides' – vacillating, egotistical, unbridled and warring – are as timely now as when they were conceived in the fifth century before Christ.

Iphigenia in Aulis is the least performed of his plays, having been described by ongoing scholars as being picturesque, burlesque and in the vein of 'New Comedy'. Nothing could be further from the truth. The story is glaringly stark – Agamemnon, head of an oligarchic army, who has lived for power and conquest, is asked to sacrifice that which he loves most, his daughter Iphigenia. He demurs but we know that the lust for glory will prevail and yet in Euripides' drama, each voice, each need, each nuance is beautifully and thoroughly rendered. Iphigenia is for the chop but at the moment when her little universe is shattered, when she realises that she is being betrayed by both God and man, she pitches herself into an exalted mental realm, the realm of the martyr-mystic who is prepared to die but not to kill for her country. It is of course, as probably in the myth surrounding Joan of Arc, a heightened, histrionic moment which pitches its heroine in the ranks of the immortals. If one of the prerogatives of art is to catapult an audience from the base to the sublime, from the rotten to the unrotten, from the hating to the non-hating, then Iphigenia does that, but her sacrifice prefigures a more hideous fate. The catharsis is brief, as the grand mechanism of war and slaughter has been set in place. Clytemnestra, the mother, helpless to avert her daughter's death, becomes an avenging fiend and ten years hence, when Agamemnon, victorious from Troy, will return with his Trojan concubine, the crazed prophetess Cassandra, he will meet a gory end at the hands of Clytemnestra and her paramour Aegisthus.

After his death in 408 BC three plays by Euripides were found – *Iphigenia in Aulis*, *Alcmaeon* and *The Bacchanals* and were put on the stage by his son, Euripides III. *Iphigenia* was incomplete and finished by another hand. The other hand is what gives the play as we know it a false and substanceless ending. At the very last moment the sacrifice is aborted, Iphigenia whisked away and a deer put lying on the ground, the altar sprinkled with the necessary blood. It seems unthinkable that an artist of Euripides' unflinching integrity, with a depth and mercilessness of sensibility, would soften his powerful story for public palliation.

History has righted his standing. The Latin poets Virgil, Horace and Ovid all acknowledged their debt to him, Plutarch would boast that he knew the plays by heart and Goëthe devoted himself to reconstructing several of his plays from fragments. He now is recognised as the greatest of that triad of Athenian giants and even his fellow countryman Aristotle, after much carping, crowned him 'that most tragic of poets'.

Edna O'Brien
January 2003

Iphigenia

For Michael Straughan who brought it to light

Iphigenia premiered at the Crucible Theatre, Sheffield on 5 February 2003. The cast was as follows:

Witch/Nurse	Joanna Bacon
Calchas/Menelaus	John Marquez
Old Man	Jack Carr
Agamemnon	Lloyd Owen
Sixth Girl	Charlotte Randle
Iphigenia	Lisa Dillon
Clytemnestra	Susan Brown
Messenger	Dominic Charles-Rouse
Achilles	Ben Price
Chorus	Kristin Atherton
(Girls, Soldiers)	Olivia Bliss
	Veejay Kaur
	Francesca Larkin
	Charlotte Mills
	Kitty Randle
	Stacey Simpson
	Rachael Sylvester
	Andrew Hawley
	Martin Ware

Director Anna Mackmin
Designer Hayden Griffen
Lighting Oliver Fenwick
Composers Ben Ellin, Terry Davies
Sound Designer Huw Williams
Choreographer Scarlett Mackmin

Scene One

A night scene, windless, hushed.

A starlit sky.

A high wall with ladders.

Witch   Great Zeus stopped the winds and why. He sends winds to other men's expeditions, winds of sorrow, winds of hardship, winds to set sail, winds to drop sail and winds of waiting but here upon the black and blasted straits of Aulis he sends no winds and an angry fleet keep asking why are we waiting, why is King Agamemnon hiding from us in his tent – because, because King Agamemnon, marshall of the fleet, made a vow to the goddess, Artemis of the sacred grove, a promise that he reneged on. Disastrous calm has driven him to augury, to Calchas the prophet who scans the flight of birds.

Spotlight on **Calchas** *the prophet.*

On the opposite side **Agamemnon** *emerges from his tent.*

The **Witch** *hides under the wall to listen.*

Calchas   King Agamemnon – to Artemis, goddess of the moon, you vowed that you would sacrifice the most beautiful you knew. You shall not unmoor your ships until you pay your dues. Your wife Clytemnestra has a child Iphigenia who in all the radiance of young beauty has been selected by the goddess Artemis to be offered in sacrifice in order that the Greek ships can leave these narrow straits for the towers and battlements of Troy. Then and only then will amorous Helen be restored to her husband Menelaus, Troy in ashes, her nobles slaughtered, her women, slave women to bring home here to Argos and plentitude of spoils.

Agamemnon   My daughter, the jewel of my heart . . . no and no and no again.

Calchas   Her mother Clytemnestra must bring her here, intended as a bride for swift-footed Achilles, son of goddess Thetis, nurtured in the watery waves.

Agamemnon   You think I would deceive my wife and child.

Calchas   The gods think it.

Agamemnon   Be gone, you old werewolf.

Calchas   Your daughter's death ensures victory for Greece.

Agamemnon   Unspeakable . . . unthinkable . . .

Calchas   In time of war, unspeakable, unthinkable things are done. For the sake of the gods and for our land thus blasted with misfortune, send for her at once and sacrifice her on the altar of divinity.

Agamemnon   Who else have you spoken to of this hatching?

Calchas   Your brother Menelaus and Odysseus of the House of Athens. The goddess Artemis, lovely lady of the woodland and the forest, is growing impatient and your men wrathful at such long waiting.

Agamemnon   I will not do it.

Calchas   It will be done.

Calchas *goes.*

Agamemnon *stands. When he turns, the* **Witch** *is in front of him.*

Witch   Hail, Agamemnon, the sacker of cities . . . the child shall have garlands put upon her head and sprinklings of lustral water. She comes to nourish with the drops of flowing blood the altar of the divine goddess from her own throat, her lovely body's throat. And grant that Agamemnon may wreathe the Hellene lances with a crown of fame and his own brows with the imperishable glory.

Agamemnon *goes.*

An **Old Man** *who has overheard pulls himself up from under the wall.*

Old Man   Dark. Darkness. The story goes of how Atreus, father of Agamemnon, had his brother's children foully and horribly slain, then boiled and served up at a banquet, all this, so that his own progeny, so that Agamemnon might rule. No one is safe. A curse is a curse. I was given as a young man with his wife Clytemnestra in all her dazzlement. I saw so much, too much. Oh, the passions, the passions; yet from great houses both were sprung.

Five wild **Young Girls** *rush in, drenched, laughing.*

Girl One   We have come through the pouring waters to see the long ships, the chariots, the dappled horses and the spear men delighting in the throw of the discus.

Girl Two   Odysseus, son of Laertes, the chieftain Adrastus, earth-born Leitus, raging Menelaus that . . .

Girl Three   . . . lost Helen to Paris the herdsman, on the mount of Ida, lured her away he did with his waxen barbarian pipe and took her to Troy.

Girl Two   And Achilles, a marvel to mortals.

Girl One   To glut our women's eyes.

Old Man   Where are your husbands?

Girl One   At home.

Girl Three   They take their pleasure at the draughts board.

They start to climb the ladders.

Old Man   Harlots. Harlots.

Agamemnon *comes out holding a book-shaped pine tablet.*

Agamemnon   Gone. Gone is every hope I had of sweetness.

He signals to a **Messenger**.

Agamemnon   Take this to my wife. Give it into her own hands. Answer no questions. Tell her to do as I command. They are awaited here and she is to bring the dowry gifts for Iphigenia to be married to Achilles. Go. Go.

The **Messenger** *goes*.

Old Man   My master, the will of the gods has swerved against you.

Agamemnon   And made me wretched.

Old Man   A king is a mortal too. Power is power, but close neighbour to grief.

Agamemnon   What would you do if it were your daughter?

Old Man   My tongue dare not answer that. A brave deed, yet a fearsome one. The child will need to pray at the shrines along the way.

Agamemnon (*gravely*)   She will.

The **Old Man** *goes*.

A sixth **Girl** *enters*.

Agamemnon (*to the constellations*)   What star are you and you and you? Do you shine into my child's bedroom where she sleeps innocent of all that will befall her? Send her a dream, tell her not to come here, tell her in language that befits her unschooled ears.

He crosses to a single star.

Agamemnon   And what star are you?

Sixth Girl   Sirius . . . still high in the heavens.

Agamemnon *turns sharply*.

Agamemnon   Who are you?

Sixth Girl   A stranger woman.
Sirius . . . sailing near the seven Pleiads the sisters, seven in
number, Electra, Maia, Taygete, Alcyone, Merope,
Celaeno, Sterope, whom Orion pursued, but they fled
before him and Zeus, pitying them, placed them in the
heavens. Only six are ever seen . . . the seventh hides in the
bosom of the sky.

Agamemnon   Come here for what?

Sixth Girl   For what I find.

Agamemnon   Where is your husband?

Sixth Girl   Dead. Killed in the first strike of the war . . .
on a small boat . . . sent out to reconnoitre in answer to the
command of raging Menelaus. Goaded to frenzy on account
of losing Helen.

Agamemnon   A good husband?

Sixth Girl   A soldier good and bad.

Agamemnon   So you have heard of Helen.

Sixth Girl   Of course. The legend of how young men went
as suitors to Sparta . . . all desiring her . . . each one
threatened to murder the other if he was successful, so when
Menelaus of the House of Atreus won her, he made a pact
with all the others that if she should ever be taken, they
would all band together and fight. But Paris with Aphrodite's
help put the dart of love into her on Ida's mountain among
the white heifers and brought her thence to Troy. It is why
we are at war and why the thousand ships out there are
manned for passage. They say that even old Hector, the
father of Paris, worships her . . . walks with her in the palace
halls, bowing and discoursing like a young gallant.

Agamemnon   But you would see her dead for your
husband's sake.

Sixth Girl   I would not. I would curry favour with her
and verse myself in all her wiles. Women can learn

marvellous things from captivating women. I have told you
my history . . . tell me yours . . . away from the main fleet
. . . here in your own quarters . . . you must be high up.

Agamemnon   Would you like me to say that I am?

Sixth Girl   Of course.

Agamemnon   That I am King?

Sixth Girl   Of course . . . every woman desires a king.

Agamemnon   Do they speak of King Agamemnon in
your village?

Sixth Girl   Ah no. The women speak of Achilles, the
handsomest of all the Achaeans, who races in full armour on
sand and shingle, racing against a four-horse chariot, lap
after lap until the horses fall down in defeat.

Agamemnon   Which would you rather look on, Achilles
or the King?

Sixth Girl   It depends. It may be that the King is old and
past his prime.

Agamemnon   What if I said that I were King?

Sixth Girl   You, him? I would fall at your feet. King
Agamemnon, leader of the Armada . . . supreme
manoeuvrer of ships . . . respected in heaven . . . worshipped
on earth . . . born for greatness . . . for war . . . for love of
women . . . O great one . . . far from home . . . no soft bed
. . . to lay your limbs on . . . turning this way and that in the
night . . . duties to weigh you down . . . do you not
sometimes wish you were a common man?

Agamemnon   I wish it now.

Sixth Girl   So we are equals.

He picks her up. In that embrace they go.

*Off-stage the sounds of very young girls singing and playing a noisy
game.*

Scene Two

Early morning.

Iphigenia*'s chamber, where she and five* **Girls** *(two of whom are her sisters) are having a pillow fight. They speak in a made-up inexplicable language, running in and out, the feathers from the pillows falling through the air.*

A **Nurse** *comes in.*

Nurse   The Queen. The Queen.

They stop instantly.

Clytemnestra *enters.*

Iphigenia   We're sorry.

Clytemnestra   Sorry?

Iphigenia   We won't do it again . . . we got carried away.

Clytemnestra   Dress yourself.

Iphigenia   Oh, Mother . . . it's only fun.

Clytemnestra   Your father wishes you at Aulis. We are to leave immediately.

Sister   We are!

Clytemnestra   Not you.

Iphigenia   I knew Father would miss me . . . every night just before I sleep I say to the brightest star – 'Please tell the King that Iphigenia misses him and is very lonely in this big palace without him . . . tell him to come home.'

Clytemnestra   Dress yourself.

Iphigenia   Mother . . . I would miss you almost as much. Did you not sleep . . . had you a bad dream?

Clytemnestra   You are to be married.

Nurse   Praise be to Zeus, Pelius, Hera and Aphrodite.

Clytemnestra   To Achilles of Thessaly.

Iphigenia   Who is he?

Nurse   Son of the goddess Thetis and a mortal father Peleus, nurtured in the watery waves of the sea.

Iphigenia   Is it true, Mother?

Clytemnestra   The letter says so.

Iphigenia   Why has he chosen me . . . he's never seen me.

Clytemnestra   You are a king's daughter . . . that is enough.

Iphigenia   And I will take my stand in the dances and the nuptial feast . . . whirling round and round for three days and three nights . . . Achilles will be in his own tent and on the fourth morning he will be led to me and I will sit there veiled until my bridesmaid slowly lifts it and Achilles gazes into my eyes. I wonder what colour eyes he has.

Nurse   Sea eyes, no colour and every colour.

Sister   Can I come?

Clytemnestra   No . . . Iphigenia and baby Orestes and I will travel . . . the rest of you remain here.

Sister   She gets everything.

Clytemnestra   You will have a husband, in time.

Sister   I want him now.

Nurse   Hush, child, hush . . . this is her day.

Clytemnestra *goes.*

The **Nurse** *unfolds a corset.* **Iphigenia** *lifts her arms for her nightgown to be taken off, the* **Nurse** *pulling tightly on the corset strings.*

Iphigenia   Ouch. Ouch. I can't breathe . . .

Sister   What does he look like?

Nurse *continues dressing* **Iphigenia**.

Nurse   He has a coat of arms made of gold, given him by his mother. The story is known throughout, in Lesbos, Tenedos, Chryses and Cilla, in all Apollo's cities and Skyrus too, how the nereid who was his mother took him down as a baby to the River Styx and submerged him in the water to protect him from all injury and so he was except for the little heel which she had held him by . . . then fearing he might be killed in the wars she had him dressed as a girl and hid him in the palace of a king who was her friend, where he lived among the king's daughters, but, one day a peddler came in to the palace forecourt with a tray of trinkets, ribbons and scarves plus a spear and a shield and while all the girls loved the fallals, Achilles picked up the spear and the peddler, who was really the scheming Odysseus dressed in rags, saw the young boy's excitement and had a servant shout out an alarm to say the palace was under attack, whereupon Achilles tore off his woman's clothing and rushed to defend the gates and so Odysseus knew he had come to the right palace and Achilles was recruited into the Greek army, given noble rank and a vast host to command.

Iphigenia   He might change his mind when he sees me.

Nurse   Fate, my little one . . . the tiny threads of fate from heaven's loom, ordained this . . . This.

Girl   What else, nurse?

Nurse   They say, that at the sight of him hearts are transformed.

Girl   How?

Nurse   I daren't say.

Iphigenia   How?

Nurse   I lack the words, child.

Girl   What else?

Nurse   His taste is to be solitary . . . he only shows himself for the tournaments and the championships and he always wins, being half a god.

Iphigenia   Will you miss me?

Nurse   More than I would my own children. The night you were born a rayon of gold shot across the sky, my name was the first name you said . . . not your noble mother Clytemnestra and not your noble father Agamemnon.

Sister One *has taken out a veil yards long, is winding it around herself, both showing off and treading on it.*

The **Nurse** *rushes and takes it back.*

Nurse   You mustn't tear it . . . it's her wedding veil . . . it's sacred.

Sister One   Achilles might prefer me to her.

Girl One   You're jealous.

Sister One   It's you that said she was a sly one coaxing the Queen.

Girl One   I did not.

Iphigenia *lets out a cry – her menstrual blood has started to flow, running down her legs.*

Sister One   Oh, look. Look.

Nurse   Sweet Iphigenia . . . sweetest Iphigenia . . . you mustn't cry . . . this husband of yours has secured the rarest prize . . . a girl just become a woman . . . a treasure.

The **Nurse** *rocks* **Iphigenia** *in her arms and sings a soft lullaby as she leads her away.*

The **Girls** *lie on the floor on their bellies and one starts a pre-wedding hymn, gradually the others join in and slowly with balletic precision they make their way on their bellies along the stage and off.*

Change of light.

Two **Chorus Girls** *enter.*

Chorus Girl One
    I passed along by the grove of Artemis
    Whose shrine is in the hollow of the hill.
    Shelter of Leto's travail
    Soft tossed palms
    The sweet laurel and silver swill of olive
    The earth red-hued, stained
    From much sacrifice.
    Overhearing that
    I would rather not speak of.

Chorus Girl Two
    The Danaan warriors
    The oared ships of the Argives
    The fleet of Ajax
    The breezes soon
    To fill the sails
    To plough the unfriendly sea
    To the walls of Troy
    For the greatness of war is great.

Sixth Girl   Caring nothing for sacrifice.

Scene Three

The sound of men shouting, disputing, off-stage on the other side of the wall.

Sixth Girl *is by a little brazier where she is boiling eggs in a long narrow saucepan.*

Agamemnon *emerges.*

Sixth Girl *takes boiled eggs from the saucepan, haws on them and cracks them on the ground. She offers one to* **Agamemnon**, *who eats it with relish.*

Agamemnon   This . . . husband . . . of yours?

Sixth Girl   What about him?

Agamemnon   What about him . . . did you give him boiled eggs?

Sixth Girl   Sometimes . . . if we had any . . . The morning he left I did because he was on a grand expedition.

Agamemnon   And now, you're giving me boiled eggs . . . is that a . . . (*Instead of the word he traces her lips.*) Little serpent.

She starts to dance. He joins her in the dance but is not as carefree with the steps as she. She darts up the ladder.

She peers over the wall and looks down, then turns back.

Sixth Girl   These soldiers of yours . . . they're mad . . . they want to kill kill kill.

Agamemnon   I cannot stop them.

Sixth Girl   If you cannot, who can?

Agamemnon   I play the role expected of me.

Sixth Girl   O . . . King.

Agamemnon *turns away, sits and starts writing on the tablet.*

Sixth Girl   Are you writing to me?

Agamemnon   No. (*Pause.*) To my daughter.

Sixth Girl   Is she beautiful?

Agamemnon   Yes.

Sixth Girl *squats and stares directly at him.*

Sixth Girl   Teach me the ways of the court . . . how to
dance and be a lady.

Agamemnon   There is no time.

Sixth Girl   Don't send me home . . . there is no one there
for me . . . Only rock and goats.

Agamemnon   You can't stay here . . . it's too dangerous
. . . my men spy and gossip and would make trouble for us.

Sixth Girl   I will find a hole where I can hide and
sometimes you will send for me.

Agamemnon   What makes you so sure that I will send for
you?

Sixth Girl   Because the blood wills it.

He kisses her. She goes.

Sixth Girl   A king. A king.

Agamemnon *goes back to his letter.*

Old Man *comes in.*

Old Man   A father again . . . you have kindled your heart.

Agamemnon   Sshhh . . . these walls have ears.

Old Man   You can trust me . . . I am a faithful friend.

Agamemnon   Find me a messenger.

Old Man   My son . . . the fastest boy in all of Argos.

Agamemnon   When you give it to him, tell him to learn
it by heart in case he is set upon by thieves.

Old Man   Teach it to me, master . . . we do not have your learning.

Agamemnon
I send you this tablet, O daughter of Leda.
In lieu of the former.
Do not come to Aulis with the girl.
The wedding celebrations are no longer.
We shall feast our daughter's wedding another time.

The **Old Man** *murmurs it after him then hides the tablet under his jacket.*

Agamemnon   When he comes to a fork in the road, tell him to look in all directions in case they have already set out. If so, tell him to turn the carriage, the horses towards Atreus, to pilot them hence. Speed, speed.

Agamemnon *goes.*

Witch *(from her bastion)*   The gods are not fooled.
Upon the battlements of Troy and around its walls the Trojan guard now stand, but soon from over the sea the goodly ships of Argos will draw into the channels of Simois to wreak slaughter. When Agamemnon has cut the head of Paris from his neck and has overturned that city there will be gnashing and tears among the maidens and wives. Lydian ladies in their golden robes cursing Helen, child of the long-necked swan, cause of all their disasters.

A **Man** *shouting off-stage. Hearing it the* **Witch** *hides herself once again as* **Menelaus** *pushes the* **Old Man** *on-stage.*

Old Man   My master will make you pay for this.

Menelaus   Traitor. Lackey.

Old Man   I serve Agamemnon and none other . . . unbind me.

Menelaus   I should bloody you here and now.

Agamemnon *appears.*

Old Man   Master. He snatched the letter from my hand as I walked to my son's hut . . . broke the seal and read it like a thief.

Menelaus   Oh, brother.

Agamemnon   Hand it over.

Menelaus   Not before I show it to my comrades.

Agamemnon   I am in command . . . I rule the army . . . I give orders.

Menelaus   Rule! You are ready to ditch them for your own crooked ends.

Agamemnon *grabs the wooden tablet and smashes it in rage.*

Menelaus   They should see you now in dread and shame, trying to cover your tracks . . . remember how eager you were to curry favour, to be their commander . . . clasping every hand, keeping open house for every citizen to visit you . . . high and low all welcome.

Agamemnon   And still are.

Menelaus   Phfff. You hide behind walls . . . you are seldom seen . . . when trouble started you showed yourself a man of straw . . . your ships were grounded and what solution did you arrive at – disband the army . . . send them home and only then did you come to me pleading, 'What am I to do? What am I to do?', and when I suggested Calchas the prophet you rejoiced and when he told you the ships would sail if your daughter would be sacrificed you agreed after a few fatherly tears and sent a letter and slept on it and sent another – traitor, coward. The Trojan barbarians will not be assailed for the very simple expedient of you and your daughter's happiness. You are not a king.

Agamemnon   Nor you a brother.

Menelaus   A weakling.

Agamemnon   You call me that but what are you – a cuckold, a husband unable to keep his wife . . . something I am not charged with . . . no woman makes me wanting in the eyes of the world. You crave Helen back for lust or pride, or both, your so-called love of Greece, your great heroics a mere ploy that hides your basest need. I will not kill my child to fulfil your urges.

Menelaus   Nor will our plans be scuttled . . . a wind will blow us safe unto Troy's coast.

The young **Messenger** *from Scene One rushes in.*

Messenger   My lord, Clytemnestra the Queen has just arrived. She was supported from her chariot holding the baby Orestes lest she stumble. Soft maidenly arms reached up to receive your daughter Iphigenia so that she would not be frightened by so many strangers. They are now bathing, the fillies let loose to drink and the army are asking, asking, because a rumour has spread that the young girl has come.

Agamemnon   What rumour?

Messenger   They gape to catch sight of the golden young girl and ask why has Agamemnon sent for her, is it that he misses her or is it that some marriage has been arranged for her by Artemis, goddess of Aulis. They shout, let there be a wedding to relieve the wretched waiting hours, let the pipes sound in the tents, let the earth thud with dancing feet, they are happy at the maiden's arrival . . . some see in it a deliverance.

Agamemnon   Run and see if they are still bathing or if they are on their way towards the house.

The **Messenger** *runs off.*

I am undone. (*To* **Menelaus**.) What shall I say to my wife? How shall I receive her? What expression shall I assume? And my little daughter? It is when she pleads with me that I will break. Argument such as her mother excels in, merely hardens my resolve, but pleading . . . Iphigenia pleading, her trusting eyes, her innocence, no father should be asked for this.

Menelaus Give me your hand.

Agamemnon Take it. For you there is victory, for me a compact with ruin . . .

Menelaus By my father and yours, by Atreus who begot us, by the gods and goddesses, I see the tears that drop from your eyes and I am not your enemy. I withdraw the harsh words I spoke. It is not right that you should suffer this agony – I do not want your child to die. Am I to win Helen back by losing my brother's loyalty – no. Or sacrifice my brother's child – no. What has Iphigenia to do with all this – nothing. Let us disband the army, let them leave these bitter straits of Aulis, scatter their ships and go home. I say this out of love for a brother and a deeper honour than winning back a faithless wife. I will search for her myself and drag her back to our homeland by her cursed hair.

Agamemnon I welcome your words as a loyal brother, but make no mistake we have come to a point where necessity dictates our misfortune. We must carry out this bestial command.

Menelaus Who is forcing it?

Agamemnon The army.

Menelaus They do not know of it yet. Send her back . . . go down to the fast-flowing stream and tell your wife the marriage with Achilles was something you dreamed, a father's folly for his child.

Agamemnon Calchas will tell.

Menelaus Not if he is dead.

Agamemnon By whose hands?

Menelaus Ours.

Agamemnon   To kill a seer invites great disaster and moreover Odysseus knows, that wily cur. Already I can see him standing before the army telling them how I proved false. He will carry them with him and for good measure allow them to kill us all . . . you, me and my entire family. Even if we escaped they would follow us, destroy our city, our palace with its immemorial walls, our household and our tribe. She shall be sacrificed.

Menelaus   When?

Agamemnon   Immediately – while this madness reigns over me. One favour, keep my wife away until it is done.

Over their speech stones have been thrown from beyond the wall and mutinous voices heard.

Put an end to their brawls. Tell them to save their murderous rage for the hosts of Troy . . . for we are presently to sail to that Phrygian land.

Menelaus   Oh, my poor brother . . . Oh, my poor king.

Agamemnon   As a broken king I go to war.

Menelaus *goes.*

Agamemnon *hits his head against the wall, again and again, violently.*

A stone is thrown over which almost hits him. He picks it up, looks at it and throws it back.

Women's voices off-stage.

Agamemnon *rushes into his tent.*

Clytemnestra *enters. She turns back to give instructions to a maid.*

Clytemnestra   Put the baby down . . . rock him . . . the journey has made him fidgety, and take the dower gifts and carry them into the house, lay them carefully.

Iphigenia *runs in.*

Agamemnon *in soldier's attire emerges.*

Iphigenia   Father, Father.

Clytemnestra   My most reverent king, we are come and we are glad to come.

Screaming of the baby off-stage.

Clytemnestra *goes off.* **Iphigenia** *holds flowers.*

Iphigenia   Smell. I picked them specially for you. When we were leaving my sisters clung to me, they wanted to come. You are strange, more than strange, what has happened, has this war made you so distant, so cold.

Agamemnon   The war has not even begun. We are paralysed. The ships are stuck out there idle . . . no winds to lift the sails.

Iphigenia   Blow the winds blow, ho the winds ho . . . You're not happy to see us.

Agamemnon   Happy. Yes yes.

Iphigenia   Take away that frown, Father. You've been separated from us too long and we from you. I've made this huge embroidery for you . . . a lamb in a meadow. It has twenty shades of gold . . . Guess how I got them . . . guess guess, I followed the turning of the sun from dawn until sunset. It hangs in the great hall, just as you come in. You can't miss it. We were so lonely without you and little Orestes does not know his father but guess what, I taught him to say your name . . . he has eight words in all, eight baby words and a lisp. There are tears in your eyes.

Agamemnon   The time is not good.

Iphigenia   Forget war . . . give it up . . . send the men away . . . come home with us . . .

Agamemnon   If I could I would.

Iphigenia   Where is Achilles? Is he in your tent waiting? What shall I say to him? What shall he say to me? Does he have a little beard? Is his voice from down here? . . . Is his armour really gold . . . Answer me, Father, answer me.

Agamemnon   There is no answer.

Iphigenia   I believe you're jealous . . . that's why you're sulking.

Agamemnon   Shut up.

Iphigenia *looks at him appalled. He has never shouted at her before. She runs off.*

Clytemnestra   You have made her cry . . . why such a mood, such shiftiness?

Agamemnon *turns and climbs the ladder to escape.*

Clytemnestra *follows and pulls him back.*

Clytemnestra   Of course you hate to lose her, but think what I feel . . . I too will feel the pangs when I lead her along the steps to the marriage grove. Yet marriage is a great thing and we should welcome it. Tell me his character.

Agamemnon   Reserved. He is quite reserved. Chiron, it is said, reared him under the sea waves so that he should not learn wickedness from men.

Clytemnestra   Excellent. So no fault is to be found in him.

Agamemnon   He sits apart from all the others . . . aloof.

Clytemnestra   It is good. It is very good . . . where does he come from . . . from which city of Thessaly?

Agamemnon   Phthia, by the River Apidanus.

Clytemnestra   Blessing on them both. Which day are they to be married?

Agamemnon   When the moon comes full round.

Clytemnestra   That is lucky.
Where shall I make the wedding feasts for the women?

Agamemnon   Down on the shore. But better leave all that to me.

Clytemnestra   Why?

Agamemnon   Lady, you will do as I say.

Clytemnestra   I am used to doing what you say . . . in everything . . . have you forgotten. And you have not kissed me. Are you afraid your men will think you weak?

Agamemnon   Go back home and take little Orestes with you.

Clytemnestra   What! Be absent from my daughter's wedding! Who will raise the bridal torch, who will say the prayers, who will crown her?

Agamemnon   I will.

Clytemnestra   That is not the usual style. A mother does these things . . . it is her privilege.

Agamemnon   I do not want you mingling with this rabble of soldiers.

Clytemnestra   I shan't mingle . . . I shall be with my husband, in his tent, under his protection.

Agamemnon   Obey!

He grips both her hands to convey his resolve.

She starts to bite his hands to free her own; the bite is both erotic and determined.

Clytemnestra   Your wife has missed you. A mother loves her children but a wife hankers for her husband once they have been put down to sleep. And have you not felt the same absence?

Agamemnon   I am at war.

Clytemnestra   War. War. War. Why are men so enamoured of war?

Agamemnon   Go and tell her that I am sorry . . . leave
me to settle something that must be settled. Patience,
Clytemnestra . . . patience.

Clytemnestra   Is there something . . . fatal?

Agamemnon   No, no.

Clytemnestra *leaves.*

Agamemnon   And so I plot and weave and slither against
her that I love so dearly.

He goes.

Clytemnestra *enters.*

On her way **Sixth Girl** *passes under the wall – they exchange a
look.*

They both go.

Agamemnon *comes out and goes to the ladder.*

A huge stone is thrown and again he picks it up and throws it back.

He climbs the ladder.

Music swells the stage as a procession of **Young Girls** *comes on
slowly, chanting a wedding song. They circle the stage.*

Witch
  To the strains of the Lythian lotus pipe
  Daughters of Nereus gather
  To stamp their golden sandals
  On the earthen floor
  For the wedding of Achilles, son of Peleus
  His suit of gold mail
  A gift
  From his divine mother Thetis.
  Daughters of Nereus join to crown
  Iphigenia's tresses.
  Iphigenia, a young heifer undefiled,
  (*Shrieks.*) is for the knife.

The **Young Girls** *go inside and the music continues within.*

Scene Four

Clytemnestra *enters, goes in search of* **Agamemnon**.

When she comes out, **Sixth Girl** *is waiting for her.*

Sixth Girl   May I speak with you.

Clytemnestra   Who are you?

Sixth Girl   A woman (*pause*) that befriends her sex.

Clytemnestra   Really! And follows the camp to pick the leavings.

Sixth Girl   My bed was cold. I lost a husband on account of Helen. Something is being kept hidden from you.

Clytemnestra   What?

Sixth Girl   Your daughter is to be sacrificed in order that they can hoist the sails and make war on Troy.

Clytemnestra   You rave.

Sixth Girl   Unhappy lady . . . you will wish you had let me into your confidence and opened that haughty heart of yours.

Sixth Girl *goes.*

Achilles *in full armour comes down the ladder.*

Clytemnestra *draws aside.*

Achilles   Agamemnon, captain of the army, Achilles stands before your door . . . the men grow fierce . . . they curse . . . their murmurs swell. 'How long more, how long more for the voyage to Ilium. What does Agamemnon intend to do, send us home.' Wreak shame on the House of Atreus and leave an army in perpetual desolation.

Over his speech the **Old Man** *has come on from one side and* **Clytemnestra** *from the other.*

Clytemnestra   Achilles, prince of greatness.

Achilles How is this – a woman . . . So stately and so fair.
Revered lady . . . this is no place for a woman, fenced in by
an undisciplined mob.

Clytemnestra I am Clytemnestra, wife of the King and
mother of Iphigenia.
Why do you run . . . join hands with me . . . as a happy
prelude for the bridals.

Achilles Touch your hand! I could not face Agamemnon
if I touched that which I have no right to.

Clytemnestra I admire your constraint, Achilles, son of
the sea, but you are to marry my daughter Iphigenia, so we
are already joined are we not?

Achilles Madam, you talk like a storybook.

Clytemnestra So formal on the brink of wedlock. Why?

Achilles Wedlock?

Clytemnestra To Iphigenia.

Achilles I have not courted your daughter Iphigenia and
marriage is far from my mind. Ten thousand girls hunt for
marriage with me, but I am a soldier first and last.

Clytemnestra I am sorry if I have overstepped – I am
mortified. I took you for my son – an empty hope. You say
you are not marrying her, an evil omen for her, for all.

Clytemnestra *goes to leave.*

Old Man Lady, I hold you dear. Your father pledged me
to watch over you in danger.

Clytemnestra Not now . . . That youth has irked me.

Old Man With cause. Don't blame him.
O Gods, save those I once saved. Save the seed of
Agamemnon. A horrible deed is contrived, we are undone.

Clytemnestra Riddles.

Old Man   The father that begat Iphigenia is going to kill her . . . to sacrifice her on the altar to Artemis.

Clytemnestra   You're out of your mind.

Old Man   It's what the girl from across the straits tried to tell you. All is prepared, the altar, the meal cakes, the cups for the blood . . . he will slit the child's throat with a sword before the sun goes down.

Clytemnestra   You are mad.

Old Man   No. The King is mad.

Clytemnestra   Why would he do this?

Old Man   Oracles. Oracles . . . so the army can sail to Troy and Helen be brought back restored to Menelaus.

Clytemnestra   How do you know?

Old Man   I was sent with a second letter to you, in lieu of the first, it said, 'Do not come to Aulis, do not bring Iphigenia here.' Menelaus met me and intercepted it . . . he is behind it . . . so is the prophet Calchas and crafty Odysseus . . . Achilles was a husband in name only, the marriage promise was a snare.

Clytemnestra   I think I see.

Achilles   I should not have spoken to you as I did. My pride was pricked. I am sometimes hasty.

Clytemnestra   As befits a warrior.

Achilles   Your husband used my name and fame for his own base ends.

Clytemnestra   Think how I feel, drawn in by his honeyed wooing, a wife of many years, this child is an angel, she thinks her father supreme above all.

Achilles   He will not succeed in this malevolent scheme.

Clytemnestra I fear it is already commenced. He left here hurriedly, no doubt to confer with Calchas the prophet.

Achilles Prophets serve their own interests, they say what suits the moment.

Clytemnestra Yet they can wreak magic too.

Achilles Let Calchas wreak good magic then.

Clytemnestra I am at your mercy. Guide me.

Achilles Act cunningly. When he returns draw him out as to what is weighing upon him, do it with your old sweetness, say you have observed his gloom, bring him round to a better mind.

Clytemnestra And then?

Achilles Together you will find a way to spirit her off to safety.

Clytemnestra What if we are not together but more divided?

Achilles As I live, I shall save the girl.

Clytemnestra O prince of princes, can that be true?

Achilles The army respect me, despite my young years. I will convene the generals, they are not fiends, they are not gutless knaves.

Clytemnestra Would it not be better if you spoke with him in all your prestige?

Achilles Not yet. My place in the army must not be compromised. Take the course I counsel.

Clytemnestra If I fail . . .

Achilles Then you may send for me.

Clytemnestra You are aware how cruel he can be, how ruthless?

Achilles   I was not brought up to flinch in the face of
danger. I no longer see him as my master, for I am his.

Clytemnestra   For you I garlanded her, I brought her
here for you. Let me ask you one last thing – see her and
your heart will melt, so young, so shy, so modest, so full of
trust.

Achilles   Do not bring her into my sight – a soldier does
not court the things that make him weak.

Clytemnestra   You will save her from death?

Achilles   I have said so.

Achilles *goes up the ladder.* **Clytemnestra** *watches.*

The music and revels from inside grow louder.

Agamemnon *appears on the top rung of the ladder.*

The **Old Man** *goes.*

Agamemnon *comes down.*

Agamemnon   They are singing within.

Clytemnestra   Indeed . . . singing *and* dancing.

Agamemnon   They seem very merry.

Clytemnestra   And you . . . you seem solemn . . . would
it not help to unburden yourself . . . to let me know of this
gravity.

Agamemnon   Where do I begin. The yoke of
circumstance . . . here in Aulis I am not a free man . . . a
violent rage, a supernatural rage possesses them.

Clytemnestra   And has infected you. You have a notion
to kill your own daughter.

Agamemnon   Who said such a thing? Who dares accuse
me of this?

Clytemnestra   It is written across your face. The
moment we arrived I saw that some dreadful constraint was

upon you . . . the way you twisted and turned and could not look in my eye or in hers.

Agamemnon   Whoever spread this rumour shall be mortally punished.

Clytemnestra   Isn't one death enough to contemplate in one day, your own daughter's at that. Who will draw the sword across her child's neck?

Echo of 'Who will draw the sword across her child's neck' *twice*.

Agamemnon   I will.

Clytemnestra   Who will slit it?

Echo of 'Who will slit it' *once*.

Agamemnon   I will.

Clytemnestra   Who will hold the cup for the . . . torrent of blood?

Agamemnon   I will.

Clytemnestra   The blade will fall from your hand.

Agamemnon   Others will raise it up.

Clytemnestra   Others. Lesser men. Menials. Stand up to them, show courage, or are you so eager to parade your sceptre and play the general.

Agamemnon   I do not count her wise, a wife, who when her husband is on the rack goads him further. Think what I have been through, think of how I have suffered, tossed from love to duty and back again, like a flotsam.

Clytemnestra   I will not let this happen.

Defy Artemis.

Agamemnon   Defy her and risk her greater wrath . . . murder for all of us . . . you, me, Iphigenia, the baby . . . it

is out of my hands, even though my hand will be the doer
of it.

Clytemnestra *realises that he is serious and rounds on him now,
striking him.*

Clytemnestra   You killed the child I bore from Tantalus,
you tore it from my breast and dashed it to the ground,
murderer . . .

Agamemnon   A murderer's accomplice – you came with
me, your tresses unbound.

Clytemnestra   I did it for my poor aged father's sake –
he whom you tricked with your honeyed words, the way you
tricked me.

Agamemnon   Sister of Helen, daughter of Leda, sisters in
lust.

Clytemnestra   You dare lump me in with Helen! I grew
temperate in Aphrodite's realm, a blameless wife towards
you and your household . . . I bore you children . . .
Iphigenia, her sisters and little Orestes, who is in there now
with her, two children believing themselves to be safe in
their parents' quarters, under their parents' tutelage.

Agamemnon   From the moment I received the oracle I
have been mad, mad. Phantom females dripping with blood
visit me in my sleep.

Clytemnestra   Huh. Phantom females.

Agamemnon   I love my child as much and more than
any father could.

Clytemnestra   What prayers will you utter after she is
dead. Do you think when you come home to Argos your
other children will embrace you, your wife will welcome you
back – God forbid it.

Agamemnon   Be my companion in this . . . help me.

Clytemnestra   Let Helen's daughter Hermione be sacrificed, it is only right, she too is young and fair, tell Menelaus to send for her and let her be swapped for our darling girl.

Agamemnon   Iphigenia was named as being the most pure, the one marked for godhead.

Clytemnestra   Then Achilles must save her.

Agamemnon   Achilles must not know of this.

Clytemnestra   He knows. He was here when the message was relayed to me, not by one . . . but by more than one . . . he smarted at being used as a foil . . . a mockery of his standing . . . but he gave me his word that Iphigenia will be saved.

Agamemnon   Would that she could.

Clytemnestra   Let us flee now, as a family, call the children. Let us outwit them . . . arrange for the carriage. Do it.

Agamemnon   It's no use.

Clytemnestra   You speak as if the deed is already done.

Agamemnon   It is.

From his back pocket he takes out a bloodied knife and she screams repeatedly.

I slew a lamb in preparation.

Iphigenia *runs out at hearing her mother's scream.*

Iphigenia   Mother! Why are you screaming? Are you and father arguing . . . but why, I am so happy . . . be happy with me . . . don't spoil it . . . I have been hearing about my husband . . . his feet are like the wind and he races on the shore against a four-horse chariot, lap after lap, day after day. O Mother, O Father, I thank you for giving me life, for being always so loving and so gentle with me . . . I thank you for Achilles, they say too that he sits alone, even at the

feast, he is Achilles the unreachable and I shall have to
humour him, the way I humour you . . . father.

Clytemnestra   Tell her.

Agamemnon   Iphigenia . . . child of my heart. I did not
bring you here of my own free will, nor are you betrothed to
Achilles.

Iphigenia   Why not?

Clytemnestra   Your father intends to sacrifice you to
Artemis the goddess.

Iphigenia   What a tall story.

Agamemnon   The gods have willed it.

Iphigenia   I begin to go cold.

Agamemnon *exits*.

Girls *from inside the house have come out to listen*.

Iphigenia   Let's get Orestes and run away.

Clytemnestra   We can't . . . we are watched on every
side. I will have you escorted to Achilles' tent . . . to plead
with him.

Iphigenia   No . . . no . . . the shame is too much . . . the
shame on him and on me.

Clytemnestra   Show him how you feel . . . reveal it . . .
give him the bait and he will take it . . . he is young, virile.

Iphigenia   I can't do it, Mother.

Clytemnestra   This is no time for delicacy.

Iphigenia   My father will save me.

Clytemnestra   Your father killed my first husband
Tantalus . . . the babe of that first husband he wrenched it
from my breast and smashed it to the ground. Pray that you
do not cause me a bitterer grief.

A **Praying Girl** *comes on.*

Agamemnon *returns.*

Iphigenia   How far is Troy . . . I will come with you.

Clytemnestra   Let her hear it from your own lips . . . tell
her that she is to be slaughtered in order to bring Helen
back.

Iphigenia   I know nothing of Helen . . . I love life . . . why
would I have to die for her sake?

Agamemnon   Artemis wills it.

Iphigenia   Why would Artemis pick on me?

Agamemnon   On account of being ripe for beatitude.

Iphigenia   Beatitude.

Iphigenia *crosses to the* **Praying Girl** *muttering the word*
'Beatitude'.

Praying Girl *kneels and rings the bell repeatedly.*

Witch *starts to sway, working herself into a trance.*

Praying Girl
    So gentle are you, Artemis the holy
    So loving are you, to dewy youth to tender nursling.
    The young of all that roam the meadow
    Of all who live within the forest
    You protect
    Hear us, Artemis
    Do not have your altar stained
    With human blood.

Praying Girl *waits and they all wait.*

Sounds like thunderclaps off-stage.

Sshh. Sshh. The goddess speaks . . .

Witch *tears open her coat to reveal her goddess attire.* (**Artemis**
speaks through the **Witch.**)

Artemis
> Would that Paris had died
> On the lonely mountain where he was left
> Cast out to die on an oracle's command
> Hapless, unmothered
> Paris the shepherd lad, prince of Troy
> Would that he had died
> By the lakeside
> By the nymph-haunted fountains
> By the meadows, starry with roses
> Would that he had perished
> But no
> Beauty's queen came
> Child of the long-necked swan
> The blame for all those troubles.
> Iphigenia
> Child without blemish
> Blessed above all the maidens
> Undo these wrongs.
> The altar is well prepared
> The blood of the lamb upon the pyre
> Say your farewells
> For it is time
> For it is time
> Swap your raiment
> Revere the sacrifice
> Not with wailing
> But with prayer
> When you have fulfilled your destiny
> You shall be raised among the blessed
> And our dear land will honour you for ever
> For it is time
> For it is time.

Iphigenia *runs to her father.*

Iphigenia   Save me.

Agamemnon   I can't.

Clytemnestra   Vile Helen, I curse you now in
whosoever's arms you bask, the swan's neck I hack with
daggers, those grey dreaming eyes I gouge from their
sockets; or better still, O daughters of Nereus, bring her here
that I may maul her with my own hands.

Agamemnon   A mother in name only, harken to the
child with soothing prayer.
O golden hair, what burden Phrygia's town has laid upon
you.

Iphigenia   No, the Greeks my own people are doing it
to me.

Agamemnon   That rage of my army is not against you,
child, but a mad rage to sail to the barbarian land, to quash
them and put an end to their rape of our women . . . Greek
women . . . Greek wives . . . Greek daughters defiled. Greek
men will not permit that most loathsome of crimes. It is not
for Helen, not for Menelaus I sacrifice you, it is for Greece.
She must be free. If it is in our power, yours and mine, to
make her so, we must.

Iphigenia   It falls to me alone . . . without you.

Agamemnon   It does.

Iphigenia   If I had Orpheus' eloquence . . . the voice to
charm the rocks . . . if I could bewitch with words, I would
bewitch now . . . but I only have tears and prayers . . . and
these I offer . . . like a suppliant . . . O Father, I press against
you now . . . this body of mine . . . which my mother bore
. . . do not destroy me before my time . . . I love the light . . .
do not despatch me down to the nether world . . . hell is
dark and creepy and I have no friends there . . . I am your
child . . . I basked in your love . . . the little games we played
. . . you would close the folding door and I would squeak
squeak and you would come back in with sugar plums and
put them under my pillow . . . you were never cross with me
. . . never haughty . . . never the King . . . I could coax you
out of your moods and when you grew a beard, I studied it

. . . I counted the hairs, I pulled on it and clung to you as I cling to you now, my first and last and only hope. In your old age I will welcome you into my own house with my own husband – whoever he be – I will have children to lighten your weary heart . . . look at me . . . give me a kiss . . . at least let me have that as a memory of you . . . if I am to . . . if I am to die.

Soldier *rushes in.*

Soldier   The anger of heaven is nothing to the anger of men. They had heard that Achilles wanted to save the young girl and they leaped upon him, seizing him by his helmet, swung him from his feet and as the first stone was thrown, a hail of stones were aimed at him to decapitate his head from his neck.

Menelaus *comes in during his speech.*

They would have killed him but that Odysseus said that even if Achilles had turned coward the sacrifice would be performed and so a few of his men that were loyal to him made a wall before him and took the stones.

Agamemnon   Did his own guard not save him?

Menelaus   They were the first to turn against him – they called him lovesick because he pleaded for the girl.

Achilles *is carried in in the arms of two bodyguards.*

Praying Girl   O healer Phoebus, make great Achilles well again.

Girl Two   Thetis, come down and save your godly son.

Iphigenia *crosses and stands over him. She begins to take out the stones from his wounds. This is the turning point for her.*

Soldiers *have climbed on the far side of the wall, calling her name.*

Agamemnon   Get Odysseus to fend them back . . . tell him that . . .

Menelaus   Tell him what?

Iphigenia   I will die.

Let me save Hellas if that is what the gods want. What is one life compared with thousands. I will do it gloriously . . . I will put frightened thoughts out of my head.

Achilles   Shining one.

Iphigenia   Don't stir.

Achilles   I swore to save you.

Iphigenia   You will be my chariot on the path across . . .

Achilles   I will die with you.

Iphigenia   And fail Greece – no. You risked your life for me and that is everything.

Achilles   Iphigenia . . . Pure star of our destiny.

Clytemnestra *slaps* **Iphigenia** *on the face to put sense into her.*

Iphigenia   Mother, I am happy . . . and one must not love life too much.

Clytemnestra   Child's talk . . . babble . . . you do not know what this means.

Iphigenia   I do know (*Pause.*) it is the end for me. Achilles tried to save me, one against all, and now I am alone.

Clytemnestra   When the blade rips into your flesh you will cry for mercy.

Iphigenia   Pray that I don't. Pray that I draw courage from you and you from me, Mother. If we can't give each other courage, who else can? We have lived a long time since we set out from home, the horses so frisky, the morning so young. Do not cut your hair, Mother, and do not go into mourning . . . you have my sisters and little Orestes who will grow into a man.

Old Man   Diverse are the natures of the mortals, she willing to die for valour and they willing to kill.

Clytemnestra *in a last desperate attempt to hold* **Iphigenia**'s *face in her hands.*

Clytemnestra   Death is a fearful thing.

Iphigenia *kisses her mother.*

Agamemnon *stands like someone in a trance.*

Agamemnon   There will be much adornment . . . she will be bathed in yellow oils, the tawny mountain honey will anoint her body . . . she shall rest upon the cenotaph; laurels, roses and hyacinths all around her.

Clytemnestra   The man has gone mad. He speaks as if it is a wedding feast.

Iphigenia   Oh, poor Father. Oh, poor King.

Clytemnestra   Man of stone.

Agamemnon   In death I shall hold you dearer than in life.

Agamemnon *embraces her.*

Over that embrace the death ritual commences.

Menelaus *takes a sword.* **Clytemnestra** *runs to grab it from him and risks her own hand to seize it. They fight over it.*

Menelaus   Seize her.

Two men *lift* **Clytemnestra** *up and pull her backwards as she screams. One puts his hand across her mouth to muzzle her.*

Menelaus   Discord between brothers must never be allowed to fester, we are our mother's sons. She too presides above the altar of Artemis, wishing us godspeed to Ilium.

Iphigenia *is raised up and carried towards the altar.*

Agamemnon *follows.*

Agamemnon   Even now this heart breaks.

Menelaus *gives* **Agamemnon** *the sword.*

Death shrieks — all female.

The blood begins to drip.

That sound held for a moment.

A breeze gusts along the stage, raising the trampled feathers from Scene Two.

The men let go of **Clytemnestra**.

The death shrieks and music continue.

Witch   Fortunes now attained . . . the glittering seat of Atreus awash with victory.

Praying Girl (*coming out*)   The blood from her gashed throat matted the curls of her hair.

Menelaus (*coming out*)   Wise men ride their luck; they seize the chance to be great, to win fame and honour.

As he climbs the ladder he shouts triumphantly to the men.

Menelaus   Hoist the sales . . . let the trumpets blare.

Agamemnon *returns, a* **Girl** *pouring water over his bloodied hands.*

When they are washed he smells them and goes to **Clytemnestra**.

Agamemnon   Noble Queen.

Clytemnestra *stands with a cold, still loathing.*

Clytemnestra   Killed for a charm against the Thracian winds.

Agamemnon   Will you not kiss a king goodbye. A husband then . . .
Farewell. It will be long before I address you again.

Agamemnon *climbs the ladder — she does not watch.*

Clytemnestra *stands utterly still.*

Sixth Girl *wearing a veil stands a little away from her as if to ask her something.*

Girl One   There is no one left for her here.

Clytemnestra   She may follow us. Her cunning will serve some purpose.

Sixth Girl *lifts the veil, bows and goes off.*

Bloodied rain starts to fall and **Clytemnestra** *is drenched in it.*

The **Young Girls** rise vivified, climb on to the ladders, speaking the prophecy of the fate to come.

(The lines are broken up and can be given as desired.)

What all men fear.

Gold and silver brought back in the Aegean ships.

The captive women of Troy.

Cassandra, daughter of Priam, Virgin of Apollo, chosen by Lord Agamemnon to be his concubine.

In contempt of the gods and all pious feeling.

Brought back to the House of Atreus.

You will greet your war-torn husband with every appearance of delight.

Unroll the purple carpet.

Lead him to the bathhouse.

When he steps out of the bath, eager for banquet, you will come forward . . .

As if to wrap a towel about him but instead . . .

It is a net . . .

Entangled in it like a fish, Agamemnon will perish at the hands of Aegisthus, son of Thysetes and corruptor of your marriage bed.

The broad blade driven in to Agamemnon's garlanded throat.

He falls on the silver-sided bath, his brain awhirl, in death convulsion, his eyes staring in disbelief at you, at you his queen.

Will add her hand to the hand of Aegisthus and drive the blade clean home into your king's breast, exacting the full price . . .

On the thirteenth day of Gamelian.

Not troubling to close his eyeballs and wiping the blood off your hands, you will return to the feast, unafraid of divine retribution.

Clytemnestra
Sweeter to me your words
Than heaven's raindrops
When the cornland buds.

Darkness.